Men W
Repeat Themselves

Mark Russell

erbacce-press
Liverpool UK

5 Farrell Close, Melling, Liverpool, L31 1BU, UK

Cover-image courtesy of the Australian War Memorial NWA0300

erbacce-press publications Liverpool UK 2022

erbacce-press.com
ISBN: 978-1-912455-31-7

Acknowledgements

My thanks are due to the editors of the following publications where some of these poems, or versions of them, first appeared:

Anthropocene, Blackbox Manifold, Denver Quarterly, Drunk Monkeys, Five:2:One, The Fortnightly Review, Foxtrot Uniform, Glasgow Review of Books, Gutter, HVTN, Hypnopomp, International Times, The Interpreter's House, The Manchester Review, Molly Bloom, The Moth, New Writing Scotland, Palaver, The Pickled Body, Poetry Birmingham Literary Journal, Poetry Salzburg Review, The Poets' Republic, Rise Up Review, SAND Journal, The Scores, Shearsman, Stand, Structo, talking strawberries all of the time, Train : a poetry journal, Tenebrae: A Journal of Poetics, and *UCity Review.*

For George & Illa

Index

Introduction

As the leaves turned bronze and fell in the autumn of 2008, the poor old Lehman Brothers went bankrupt. Banks all over the world collapsed like children having hissy fits in a game of Jenga. This is how fragile, how infantile capitalism really is. Perhaps this is where the idea of *Men Who Repeat Themselves* was sown.

*

I have taught Brecht to senior pupils for nearly thirty years. Part of that process requires them to develop their own directorial and design ideas for a play written in 1939 as a warning to the Scandinavian countries not to sup with the devil of Nazism.

You can't study this play, I say to them, without understanding the Wall Street Crash of 1929 and its consequences, which finally exploded into World War II ten years later.

So, from 2008, I have asked them to think about the worldwide banking system being flushed down the toilet; the rise in unemployment and suicide rates; bankers' bonus payments being unaffected. How might these things serve the pupils as the basis for set or prop design, for costume or programme notes. What can this old play show us about ourselves today? Are we on a slow, unguarded, nonchalant march toward fascism and war? Is our silence a form of complicity? Perhaps this is where the idea of *Men Who Repeat Themselves* was sown.

*

Glasgow was cold and grey on 23rd January 2013. The temperature barely rose above freezing. Humidity was 85%. Enough to chill your bones and turn you blue. On that day, David Cameron promised to hold an in-or-out referendum on the UK's continued membership of the European Union. It felt like another significant step taken by the great western democracies toward the authoritarian, ultra-nationalism so many of them seemed to crave once more.

They said it was in the name of sovereignty, but it was a sovereignty the country had never lost. In reality, the whole thing had been manufactured by a handful of sickeningly rich people in order to avoid a bit of tax. It was done in the name of business. For the profit of a few public schoolboys. Of course it was. Perhaps this is where the idea of *Men Who Repeat Themselves* was sown.

And in the debates that followed, the left did almost nothing to oppose it. Because so many of them backed it, too. Because, they said, the EU was the smiling face of the evil that is global capitalism. The far right and the far left wanting the same thing. For different reasons, naturally. But they were prepared to let us all suffer while they grubbed around in the dirt to get it. This must have been where *Men Who Repeat Themselves* germinated.

*

On the 23rd June 2016, more than 17 million people in the UK voted to leave the EU. I woke that morning wanting to be sick. My stomach turned over in the way it did when my father died. It was grief. Of course it was grief. The single most important institution, the single most important article of faith that had worked long and hard to prevent (too much) war in Europe for so long, was breached. That day, fascism had fewer obstacles to the re-enactment of its grotesque ragbag of ideals.

Later that year, a bloated, narcissistic sociopath, fat on his ego and privilege, took the White House. Another slipped into the UK's Foreign Office (within three years this one would be Prime Minister). Yet another had been sitting in the Kremlin for goodness only knows how long. And there were more. Suddenly, we were awash with 21st century little Lord Haw Haws. They love a party, that's for sure. And other people's money. And sabre-rattling. And lying. Especially lying.

It hadn't taken ten years.

I could touch the green shoots of *Men Who Repeat Themselves*.

*

For some reason, best known to academics and newspaper columnists, every time the prose poem becomes popular, people are encouraged to wonder where it has come from. They are encouraged to view it as curious, errant, and lazy; to declare that a block of text with no lineation can't possibly be a poem. Men, it seems, can ignore the gentle acceptance of prose poetry in 17th century China; or that it was the cause of a gentle hoo-ha in 19th century France. Plainly, prose poetry is nothing new. But every time there is a resurgence in its use, men pretend it is. Because it creates conference papers. Because it fills column inches. And men like column inches. Column inches mean money.

*

I've searched through my old files and find that the first line of 'Men on Horses' emerged in July 2017. The next lines came the following week. Men kept going to war. Men kept lining their pockets. Men kept blaming everybody else. Men are to blame. We all know that. But they never pay the consequences. So, men didn't deserve the divisions of traditional verses. Soon there were 15 poems. Then 69. Then 154 (and then one more for luck). I began to send these prose poems containing men's repeated misdemeanours to journals and magazines. Editors started to take them. Editors clearly agreed: men are to blame. Over and over again.

So here they are now, all the men gathered together for the first time, on display in a continuous, public loop of shame. The men we love, the men we hate, and the men about whom we are completely indifferent. All these men will repeat themselves unless we stand in massed united action and put a stop to their fatuous games, to their endless arseholery.

Mark Russell June 2022

Men on Horses
(Previously published in *Tenebrae*, 2017)

About war, they say, there is nothing new to learn. It is as common to sleep, as it is to die. It is the quality of one's sleep, and by equal turns, the quality of one's death, that may cause us to reconfigure the banal. A man on a horse may be in a state of grace, or destined for the big fire. Two men on a horse may be in hopeless flight, or part of a comedy bill on a Tuesday night at the City Halls.

Men Looking Across Rivers

(Previously published in *The Scores*, 2017)

About war, they say, there is nothing left to pass on to our children. It is as common to declare friendship to a man named Albie, as it is to murder him in cold blood. It is the peculiar nature of male fellowship, and by equal turns, the way in which the location of military storage facilities are reported by the British tabloid press, that may crush our dreams. A man holding two contradictory propositions in his nonliteral hands may regard one true, one false, both true, both false, or none of the above. Two men holding two contradictory propositions in their nonliteral hands may regard the whole kit and kaboodle as futile and unnecessary given the dominance of white heterosexual men in early 21st century world affairs, or unable to count to four.

Men Visiting Bars in Salta la Linda

About war, they say, there is nothing new to chase: through the streets of a Bank Holiday city centre; across the fields of a Middle English hamlet; up the draughty staircase of an abandoned library; in and out the mystifications of the body. It is as uncommonly common to chase away the blue fug of independence debates, as it is to retain its veneer for safety. It is the changing colours of a subtropical highland sunset, and by equal turns, hope trumped by a concept sometimes known as sin, that may pray on the minds of those most terminally ill with the Fantasies. A man sipping silver listening to Sibelius may have siblings in Siberia, or be less sober than he imagines. Two men sipping silver listening to Sibelius may be amassing undeniable evidence to deny climate change, or looking forward to a Baltic cruise that coincides with the Nobel Prize awards ceremonies.

Men Who Know Love's Story

About war, they say, there is nothing new to hug and kiss. It is as common to sing of chivalry and lost notions of romantic love, as it is to thrash about in the hay with a string of 17th century shepherd boys. It is *les mots justes* of Middle English, Occitan, and Romanian, and by equal turns, *les bons mots* of those who would see us live forever in Tithonic decrepitude, that may inform our attempts to connect beyond the horrors of infatuation. A man with a penchant for concocting love potions may be a Royal Marine Commando on 24-hour shore leave, or your mother's secret *inamorato*. Two men with penchants for concocting love potions may be devils on the dance floors of Budapest, or about to fuel up the jet fighters.

Men on Call

(Previously published in *The Scores,* 2017)

About war, they say, there is everything to lose and only a few islands to gain. It is as common to wait for the music to start before putting the orange in your pocket, as it is for prevailing winds to blow in an unexpected direction. It is the density of the jungle terrain, and by equal turns, the physical attributes of the circus people, that may cause lawyers to become involved. A man seeking thrills on Solomon Islands Time may be researching an errant family ancestor, or claiming expenses from his employer for items he did not purchase. Two men seeking thrills on Solomon Islands Time may be gamers who have misread the rules of their new delivery, or completing a bucket list before they are either married or divorced (they may not be sure which is their true motive at this time).

Men Smoothing Walls

(Previously published in *Sand*, 2018)

About war, they say, there is nothing new to moderate. It is as common to deploy one's nephews to the front, as it is to settle briefly in Alaska. It is the purchase of a colour television, and by equal turns, the slow degradation of childhood memories, that may diagnose our obsession with uniforms. A man back from the front for the first time in seven years may take a lump hammer to the mirror, or refuse to recount tales of derring-do. Two men back from the front for the first time in seven years may set up a small-town painting and decorating business, or fill their waistcoats with stones.

Men Sleepwalking

About war, they say, there is nothing new for which to stay awake. Men are so excited by the prospect of old-fashioned war, they break first into a trot, just as they imagine their grandfathers' horses did, and then kick it up from canter to gallop. Men love their horses in the same way they pretend to be asleep when the washing needs to be done. Men love their good ol' wars. They don't need to be awake in order to direct the troops, the guns, the advances, or retreats. These are the same face of a fraudster's coin, anyway. Men love their horses. Men love their coins. Men love to carry torches and wear white gowns as they amble into war.

Men on Men
(Previously published in *Sand*, 2018)

About war, they say, there is nothing new to dream of. It is as common to shun delights of the flesh, as it is to devote oneself to sensuality. It is the interchangeable use of antonymous terms for 'conflict', and by equal turns, the baffling way in which Brazil is confused with Russia, that may be the root cause of the gender pay gap. A man high on amphetamines may be designing a chariot to wear on his head, or endlessly re-writing his essay on the male gaze. Two men high on amphetamines may think they are re-enacting the labours of Heracles, or enjoying themselves with stolen gin in an empty field.

Men Who Worship Athena

(Previously published in *Sand*, 2018)

About war, they say, there is nothing new for men to mistake for love. It is as common to plant olive trees in a field of remembrance, as it is to weave spiders for protection. It is the number of fragments into which a shield may be broken, and by equal turns, the colour of marble you choose for the sarcophagus, that may ignite the heavy woollen frieze in the dining room. A man dragging his enemy by the hair may feel this bloodshed will never end, or be closing in on the shlemiel who stole his trumpet. Two men dragging their enemy by the hair may be planning to introduce a Bill for debate, or peering over the wall of the girl's playground at The Sisters of Spectacular Nonsense Secondary School.

Men Disturbed in Their Toilet
(Previously published in *Poetry Salzburg*, 2019)

About war, they say, there is nothing new to insinuate. It is as common to peddle propaganda through the invention of a mythical Land of Lower Gods, as it is to peddle propaganda to oppose the Lower Gods through the invention of the kingdom of Vaster Godland. It is the prospect of growing old, and by equal turns, the prospect of dying childless, that may be the source and cause of this thirst for battle. A man with the body of a woman but the soul of a man may be the dream date of 5th century Roman commanders, or staggering home after a rave on the outskirts of Hemel Hempstead. Two men with the bodies of women but the souls of men may be delegates at a conference examining 'Shieldmaiden, Amazon, or Valkyrie: Patriarchal Definitions of Female Heroism', or standing for selection as UKIP's next candidate for a Parliamentary by-election.

Men Sent Forth as Champions
(Previously published in *Poetry Salzburg*, 2019)

About war, they say, there is nothing new to share with our neighbours. It is as common to bathe in the lake after nightfall, as it is to be born into a royal dynasty. It is the proximity of the de-militarised zone, and by equal turns, the comfort to be found in a lumpy hay bale, that may herald the acquisition of wisdom. A man caught on the stairwell scribbling in a notebook may be a life class model taking his legally entitled break, or transcribing the words of his colleagues whom he has taped without their permission. Two men caught on the stairwell scribbling in notebooks may have been chased out of their houses by barbarians, or be establishing rules for those cursed to remain on earth practising forensic psychology in the former republics.

Men Who Prize Their Daughters
(Previously published in *Poetry Salzburg*, 2019)

About war, they say, there is nothing new to adapt. It is as common to employ an instrumental ensemble, as it is to sing *a capella* at the ambassadors' dinner. It is the shape of the begging bowl, and by equal turns, the quality of your threads, that may turn the king's head. A man composing soundtracks for East German movies may lack the energy of his youth, or be troubled by his own historical collaborations. Two men composing soundtracks for East German movies may hope to discuss politics and the affairs of state in calmer circumstances, or accept that one day the prophecies to which they give no credence may well come true.

Men in the Orchestra

(Previously published in *Poetry Salzburg*, 2019)

About war, they say, there is nothing new to present at court. It is as common to fantasise about a close friend, as it is to seek help with one's addictions in yet another addiction. It is the struggle with monogamy, and by equal turns, the pitfalls of polygamy, that may re-draw the boundaries of Mesopotamia. A man who abandons his son to wolves may be trying to secure the release of his people, or misunderstanding the accepted protocols of negotiation. Two men who abandon their sons to wolves may suffer from fits, or be seeking revenge for their cuckolding.

Men Stationed at Temples

(Previously published in *Poetry Salzburg*, 2019)

About war, they say, there is nothing new to imagine. It is as common to protest to one's father that his premise for conducting torture is wrong, as it is to replace dead flowers at a graveside. It is the silence of birds, and by equal turns, a cacophony of misgivings, that may prepare us for a journey to Megiddo. A man with one broken lens in his binoculars may continually confuse wood with trees, or slowly begin to believe what he sees. Two men with one broken lens in their binoculars may take this opportunity to feel a righteous misery (and then manipulate others to join them in this emotional state) (thus raising the suspicion that they are not truly feeling this sense of misery themselves), or have come to arrest the heroes.

Men, Nonetheless
(Previously published in *Blackbox Manifold*, 2018)

About war, they say, there is nothing new to display either in public, or in the privacy of one's own home. It is as common to know the truth but forbid oneself to speak it, as it is to both love and betray the same person in the same day. It is the glint of a discarded dagger by the roadside, and by equal turns, the threat of wealth without influence, that may drive lovers, brothers, and sisters to reach for a book of old tales. A man afflicted with internal monologues may associate combat with competition, or over-knead his dough due to the distractions of celebrity fashion news. Two men afflicted with internal monologues may leave their posts undefended in the grand tradition of *Götterdämmerung* border guards, or about to humanise their foe, however unintentionally.

Men Fishing

(Previously published in *Blackbox Manifold*, 2018)

About war, they say, there is nothing new to use as bait. It is as common to be expelled from the belfry, as it is to be raised from the riverbed. It is the sight of the burning ships from the plains, and by equal turns, the sight of the plains from the burning ships, that may determine the agenda for the proposed negotiations. A man faced with the choice of losing a hand or gaining an irrepressible thirst for revenge may decide to run away to hide in the forest, or seek the counsel of bog dwellers. Two men faced with the choice of losing a hand or gaining an irrepressible thirst for revenge may limit their deliberations to seven years, or place advertisements in the local newspapers for *doppelgängers*.

Men Holding Candles
(Previously published in *Blackbox Manifold*, 2018)

About war, they say, there is nothing new to help us sleep. It is as common to be hailed for lionhearted derring-do, as it is to be executed for mutiny. It is the application of goose fat to the King's buttocks, and by equal turns, the evidence of one's old school chums, that may cause us to rue our liaisons with the lowland paramours. A man sent to protect the British Raj may be unknowingly under the influence of heavy sedatives, or convinced 'gung-ho' is a far eastern dish to be eaten with the tender shoots of the bamboo plant. Two men sent to protect the British Raj may be utterly fearless, or have been rusticated from University College, Oxford for not denying authorship of their pamphlets.

Men to Be Pistol Whipped
(Previously published in *Stand*, 2019)

About war, they say, there is nothing new from which to secede. It is as common to withdraw to the parlour for a laugh at the men's expense, as it is to withdraw to the sitting room for brandy and exploding cigars. It is the repeal of peace and friendship, and by equal turns, the ratification of grotesque ignorance, that may dynamite the educational institutions of the West. A man who claims to have the full support of the British people may wave his season ticket like a drunk in the Tilton Road stand, or be capable of digging up your grandmother, fucking her decomposing bones, strangling her to a second death, and re-burying her. Two men who claim to have the full support of the British people may be chinless, spineless, and fascistic members of Her Majesty's Government, or the cheeks of a horse's arse that have learned to speak English (figuratively speaking).

Men Riddled with Arrows
(Previously published in *Stand*, 2019)

About war, they say, there is nothing new to betray. It is as common to build a new integrated public transport network, as it is to fill the ocean with synthetic organic compounds. It is the low-level lighting of the triumphal arch, and by equal turns, the broad tree-lined avenues that lead to it, that may remove any lingering uncertainty of meaning from the bodies being washed ashore. A man highlighting the competing ideological visions for post-war Europe may have been hit on the head by an air drop of toothpaste from a Douglas C-54 Skymaster aircraft flying above Tempelhof Airport, or be a tense and over-wrought History teacher. Two men highlighting the competing ideological visions for post-war Europe may not have read the small print of the Potsdam Agreement, or be revising for an appearance on ITV's daytime quiz show The Chase.

Men Lighting Candles

(Previously published in *Blackbox Manifold*, 2018)

About war, they say, there is nothing new to crush our spirits. It is as common to surrender, as it is to charge the heavy guns. It is being placed in the custody of a Middle European count, and by equal turns, being reunited with an old cell mate, that may quell the growing discontent among the lower middle classes. A man caught *in flagrante* with Lady Hughenden may laugh it off as a silly misunderstanding, or become a laughing stock among society ladies at court. Two men caught *in flagrante* with Lady Hughenden may be acting under orders, or celebrating the recent demise of the latest Lord Hughenden.

Men Taking Precautions

(Previously published in *Stand*, 2019)

About war, they say, there is nothing new to exhaust. It is as common to hit the wall, as it is to break the tape. It is the slight lift in the heel, and by equal turns, the tautness of the running shorts, that may reduce the sperm count. A man who shaves every day may do so to gain personal and social importance, or to pay homage to his great grandfather who lies in an unmarked grave. Two men who shave every day may be in training for the Tour de France, or belong to a smooth-skinned religious sect.

Men Removing Gems from Their Owners

(Previously published in *Stand*, 2019)

About war, they say, there is nothing new to endorse. It is as common to be the earthly incarnation of radical profiteering, as it is to enjoy the calming swing of Herb Albert's Tijuana Brass while caught in the seventh month of persistent crossfire. It is the allegorical accounts of the end of the last ice age, and by equal turns, the practice of virtue in dark tunnels, that may replace the need to slay goats as sacrifice. A man who believes this is the Great War (To End All Wars!) may watch too much television, or have been hoodwinked again. Two men who believe this is the Great War (To End All Wars!) may be the first soldiers to reach the television and radio station, or pissing in each other's pockets and saying it's raining.

Men as Decorative Symbol

About war, they say, there is nothing left to run up the flagpole. Except if the flagpole is a metaphor. Which of course it is. Except if the flagpole is nothing but a metaphor. Which of course it isn't. These are common mystifications, uncommonly demystified. It is the heartache, and by equal turns, the deadline, that may be the whole point of the framing device. A man carrying a flag may be looking for a flagpole, or setting out on the journey home in his sailing ship. Two men carrying a flag may be unaware of its religious, economic, social, and geopolitical significance, or a couple of tax-dodgers on holiday near the Italian border.

Men Recording Dictation

(Previously published in *International Times*, 2019)

About war, they say, there are no new anecdotes to collect. It is as common for a personal secretary to be within hand's reach of his direct superior, as it is for him to be on overseas development work. It is the free man who insists we take account of his actions, and by equal turns, no account of his acquired status in society as the ultimate measure of his personality, that may lead to a permanent position within the Home Office. A man unable to sit his written exam papers due to a laboratory accident may be preparing to repel an invasion by the US Navy, or using the scar tissue as a means of receiving sympathy. Two men unable to sit their written exam papers due to a laboratory accident may vow to resign their posts as part-time hospital porters on ethical grounds when the conflict subsides, or dream of being promoted above their current rank of associate professor without having to do any original research.

Men in Retreat

(Previously published in *Tenebrae*, 2017)

About war, they say, there is nothing new to sell. It is as common to come upon a lost platoon of scouts in the marshes, as it is typical to be buried in the debris of a shelled outhouse (and, moreover, one in which you believed it would be safe to hide, and to which you persuaded others to follow). It is the loaded but jammed gun lying next to our temple, and by equal turns, the rancid smell of decaying flesh floating through the grocery aisles of the supermarket, that may one day force us to consider our deeds, to balance the good versus the bad, should we ever learn to distinguish between the two. One man reading mediaeval morality plays for instruction may be musing on the capricious nature of parking attendants outside the library, or dreaming of camping in the magic forest. Two men reading mediaeval morality plays for instruction may be the most recently hired interns for a literary festival, or mercenaries on the lam from a Balkan conflict posing as formally uneducated fishermen.

Men Distinguished by Feathers

About war, they say, there is nothing new to celebrate. It is as common to be ejected from the tavern well before closing time, as it is to voice one's opinions when it is clearly perilous to do so. It is the act forbidden in Leviticus, and by equal turns, the same act championed in Deuteronomy, that may ruin our weekend break in Birmingham, Alabama. A man protected by beggars may eventually go to sea to escape poverty, or become known throughout the arrondissement for his sweet singing voice. Two men protected by beggars may be highwaymen who give their spoils to the poor, or crypto-currency nutjobs moving among us like a waterborne disease.

Men in Pursuit of Amusement

About war, they say, there is nothing new to scare us witless. It is as common to ford a river using a stout pole to aid one's footing, as it is to cross a river by stolen ferry. It is the executioner disguised as a monk, and by equal turns, the monk disguised as Boudica, Warrior Queen of Britain, that may make us wet the bed well into our thirties. A man bluffing his way through a police cordon may be *en route* to meet the remaining co-conspirators, or a Domino's Pizza Delivery man looking for his scooter. Two men bluffing their way through a police cordon may be stable boys from the palace trying to establish an alibi, or interpreters from the embassy, late for their flights to Madrid.

Men, Always the Men

About war, they say, there is nothing new to cash in or out. It is as common to wear your hair long and wavy, as it is to shave it to a shiny ball of bone and flesh. It is the thumb in the belt, and by equal turns, the leather jacket over the shoulder, that may drive the other boys crazy. A man hopelessly in love with himself may deliver a beautiful rendition of the sweetest new wave song from his 80s canon over and over and over again, or, having decided he cannot repeat the rhyme 'rain' and 'pain' one more time, plunge into heroin addiction and reality television shows. Two men hopelessly in love with themselves may march on Swindon whistling a merry tune about the end of Mercian Supremacy, or spend long summer days wishing they possessed that which they do not possess.

Men Blocking Legislation

About war, they say, there is nothing new with which to dominate Europe. It is as common to cut off ties with the Romance countries, as it is to improve diplomatic ties with the Anglo-Saxons and Nordic nations. It is the non-combatant surgeons and bricklayers, and by equal turns, the pugnacious professors and their irascible students, that may animate the trolls of St Petersburg. A man who feels threatened by the presence of women in the workplace may wish for an economic downturn, or apply for a government re-training programme. Two men threatened by the presence of women in the workplace may join their local male-only golf club, or take that extra slice of pizza, slowly become plump and unattractive, and fall fatally in love with guns.

Men with Cameras

About war, they say, there is nothing new to hide in the barns of Balkan villages. It is as common to find an unconscious airman hanging from a tree by his parachute, as it is to bury food and medicine at an agreed co-ordinate east of the fallow field. It is the fear of capture, and by equal turns, the excitement of insurrection, that may ready a man for the anticipated onslaught. A man who forgets his password may have once been a major figure on the literary circuit, or have become the butt of jokes shared among his grandchildren. Two men who forget their passwords may be the only survivors of the latest futile putsch attempt, or unusually stimulated by the resetting of passwords.

Men in Moonlight

About war, they say, there is nothing new to fear. It is as common to mistake a fresh corpse for your still breathing companion, as it is utterly disgusting to leave less than a 10% tip for your underpaid waitress. It is the winged and sword-bearing youth within us, and by equal turns, his hypnotic sibling's gentle poisons, that may help to calm our hands at the point of death. One man under a waterfall has as much chance of surviving a gas attack as two men under the same or similar waterfall. Two men in a cave guarded by bears have more chance of being rescued by their own troops than one man in a cave surrounded by nothing but his own instincts.

Men Who Throw Their Voices

(Previously published in *HVTN*, 2018)

About war, they say, there is nothing new to access. It is as common for a day to last a century, as it is to last a minute. It is the wind's subtle whistling, and by equal turns, the water's terrifying weight, that may loosen our certainties. A man may walk through the woods like a seal, or steal through the sea like a bird. Two men may walk over bones in a basement, or shape their remains into castles.

Men Singing Doo-Wop

(Previously published in *Shearsman*, 2018)

About war, they say, there is nothing new to detain us. It is as common for the tenor to be on top, as it is for the bass to be on bottom. It is the chaos of harmony, and by equal turns, the peace of discord, that brings the barbershop to heel. A man insisting on using the off-beat may be passing on his DNA to all and sundry, or about to die by firing squad. Two men insisting on using the off-beat may dress like that on purpose, or to avoid capture by the bad guys.

Men with the Sun at Their Backs

(Previously published in International Times, 2019)

About war, they say, there is nothing new to give us hope. It is as common to be brutalised, as it is to make a unilateral declaration of independence and fuck the consequences. It is the food shortages, and by equal turns, the political turmoil in the North East, that may give the locals excuse to leave their English lovers. A man nicknamed Bug may be too tall and wide to poke fun at, or so small and frequently unwashed that he will forever be the butt of jokes. Two men nicknamed Bug may have identical disfigurements acquired in a trampoline accident from their days as Army Reservists, or be brothers with unimaginative friends.

Men Who Go on Night Patrol
(Previously published in *International Times*, 2019)

About war, they say, there is nothing new on which to gaze. It is as common to order pizza in the midst of the firestorm, as it is to feel the elation of adolescent adventures wane with the winter sun. It is the piquancy of repentance that will ultimately reveal the presence or absence of an Almighty, and by equal turns, the peculiar shape of a lover's buttocks, that may honk your horn like a goose on the lash. A man surveying a mining disaster may be remembering the battlefields of his youth and wishing one would replace the other, or listing his enemies in an out-of-date Filofax. Two men surveying a mining disaster may be sifting dust hoping to find gold, or preparing to perform Chekhov by playing only the subtext, to transform their own lives through the transformation of others.

Men Reading

(Previously published in *Shearsman*, 2018)

About war, they say, there is nothing new to hunt. It is as common to write a Dear John letter sitting on the beach at Big Sur, as it is to cycle through the mountains in 45°C. It is the distance between the tongue and the gun, and by equal turns, the veracity of the clinical drugs test, that may land a Tornado safely in the desert, far from centres of population. A man found reading Plato in translation in a public toilet may be a Greek scholar after all, or taking precautions. Two men found reading Plato in a public toilet may be understandably annoyed at the intrusion, or the CEOs of rival corporations that produce high performance battery packs for light civilian and military helicopters.

Men Revoking Charters
(Previously published in *HVTN*, 2018)

About war, they say, there is nothing new to compare with astrology. It is as common to arrive late to Donnybrook Fair, as it is to leave early. It is the sale of sheep and carrots, and by equal turns, the alcohol-fuelled tumult that surrounds it, that may end six hundred years of the simple life. A man telling stories in the oral tradition may be questioning his identity, or the identities of the villagers at large. Two men telling stories in the oral tradition may be performing an important ritual to maintain peace, order and social cohesion, or fomenting bigotry, ignorance and hatred in order to maintain sovereignty over the bailiwick.

Men in Mobile Field Hospitals

About war, they say, there is nothing new to fetishise. It is as common for a man to give up only his name, rank, and serial number, as it is for his captors to loosen his ties, stick on a Laurel and Hardy compilation DVD, and nip out to the pub for a quick pint. It is the nationality of the medical staff, and by equal turns, the fine detail in the military uniforms, that may determine whether he is released into Niagara or onto the Falls. A nurse taking a man's pulse may be an alien agent administering truth serum, or a highly trained health professional considering a life in Dubai. Two nurses taking a man's pulse may be a figment of the man's tired imagination, or figures of certain and robust cliché.

Men Smoking Outside Convents
(Previously published in *HVTN*, 2018)

About war, they say, there is nothing new to fill with nests. It is as common to resist wearing leg coverings, as it is to join the latest gumboot dance company busking on Edinburgh's Royal Mile. It is the smoke that turns into snakes, and by equal turns, the snakes that turn into stones, that may re-write the history of the hoi polloi. A man with the humanity to liberate others may be roundly mocked by his peers, or silenced by the venom of his yoke. Two men with the humanity to liberate others may be afraid their number is low, or prefer to get drunk down in the harbour and get new serpent tattoos inked into their calves.

Men on Leave

About war they say there is nothing left to tear to pieces. It is as common to capture spies allied to a foreign enemy, as it is to suspect oneself of treason. It is the means of travel one chooses, and by equal turns, the occupation of one's slave master, that defines a city as barbarous or civilised. A man passing secrets to the village doctor may think himself a Lost Boy, or descended from the House of Lancaster. Two men passing secrets to the village doctor may deplore the onset of Modernism, or be devising witty ways to write an instantly forgettable but extremely lucrative pop music hit for the Xmas market.

Men Falling into Debt

(Previously published in *Train*: a poetry journal, 2019)

About war, they say, there is nothing new to increase the quality of the housing stock. It is as common to massage one's figures, as it is to massage one's inner thigh. It is the rise in spending on food and healthcare, and by equal turns, the reduction in the infant mortality rate, that may obscure the level of discontent from the inspectors. A man active in local affairs may be delighted to include the Alderman and his wife as his close friends, or be raiding the church charity box late at night. Two men active in local affairs may prefer to direct rather than to act in the amateur dramatic society pantomime, or persistently request the emails of their colleagues through the Freedom of Information Act in order to mount claims for unfair dismissal and compensation on the grounds of bullying and intimidation within the workplace.

Men Aroused by Hair
(Previously published in *HVTN*, 2018)

About war, they say, there is nothing new to tempt us. It is as common to appear at dusk and follow her home from work, as it is to hide in the bushes to serenade her as she sleeps. It is the way in which she eats her fruit, and by equal turns, the mesmerising instability of the hazel in her eyes, that may lead a mule to the hitching post. A man deaf to the objections of others may forge his guitar from gold bars, or burn his banknotes in the rain. Two men deaf to the objections of others may be happily married but lack acceptable forms of self-control when out of the house, or be schooled in life-affirming actions that have no unacceptable consequences (e.g., certain kinds of traders on the floor of the Stock Exchange, Hollywood movers and shakers, men named Bob, Vicente, Conrad, Nigel, etc., who are capable of intelligent thought but prefer not to demonstrate it, scaffolders, white van drivers, professional sportsmen, unemployed, students, soldiers/sailors/airmen, bureaucrats in local government positions, civil servants in national government positions, men named Chris, Geoff, Walter, Pierre, etc., who walk their dogs at night, diplomats taking international positions without the necessary experience to further the cause of diplomacy, teachers/doctors/nurses, men named Claus, Ronnie, Aleksander, Gerard, etc., who like to wander aimlessly through the city, policemen/dress designers/helicopter pilots/, men named Antonin, Jim, Hans, Big Pete, etc., who are living comfortably on their pensions, senior lecturers in Economics, seasonal mushroom pickers, shop owners, shop workers, men named Chuck, Ibrahim, Juan, Martin, etc., who moonlight, consultants, CEOs, astronauts and cosmonauts, and others, the many others).

Men Watching Movies at the Auto-da-fé

About war, they say, there is nothing new to recognise. It is as common to be sent ahead to scout the enemy's position, as it is to take the opportunity to abscond with the General's daughter, pay for plastic surgery with the brigade's petty cash, and move to Marseilles. It is the intemperance and reckless behaviour of the untrained soldiery, and by equal turns, the wit and acuity of the local guerrillas, that may turn the town centre into a maze of ruin. A man who has never lived in an independent state may send his gold to the British / Portuguese / Chinese / Dutch / Austro-Hungarians[1] for safekeeping, or throw in his lot with the Russians / Germans / French / Japanese / Ottomans[2]. Two men who have never lived in an independent state may sit in taverns and draw up credible constitutions on beer mats to keep themselves alternately amused / miserable, or throw in their lot with the Spanish / Belgians / North Americans / Romans[3].

[1] *delete / make addition as appropriate*

[2] *delete / make addition as appropriate*

[3] *delete / make addition as appropriate*

Men Without Funds for Medical School

About war, they say, there is nothing new to place in Santa's sack. It is as common to sing carols for the poor, as it is to apologise for all the ethnic cleansing. It is the death of elves, and by equal turns, the mythologies of prisoner of war camps, that may help to sanctify the politicians. A man on trial in The Hague may feel genuine remorse and accept his punishment, or genuine justification and spit on the legitimacy of the court. Two men on trial in The Hague may hold fast to their conviction that evil is a subjective human construct designed to shroud its complete lack of empirical evidence in fairy dust, or a couple of cleaners on night shift acting out a scenario in which two white guys from the West are held to account for their actions.

Men Waiting for Dinner

(Previously published in *HVTN*, 2018)

About war, they say, there is nothing new to write on greeting cards. It is as common to sentimentalise the evacuees billeted to the country, as it is to yearn for the return of Batista and the gambling casinos of Havana. It is the cup of tea at half-time, and by equal turns, the lack of protest songs from the terraces, that may help us to ignore starvation and disease. A man made of stern stuff may find his father fascinating, or repulsive. Two men made of stern stuff may find their mothers repressive and frustrating, or little less than warring goddesses.

Men of Few Thoughts

(Previously published in *International Times*, 2019)

About war, they say, there is nothing new to divine. It is as common to repeat a lie, as it is to repeat a lie. It is the size of the rod one makes for one's back, and by equal turns, the size of the rod one makes for the backs of others, that may rock the house to its foundations. A man of sound and healthy mind may never need assistance from his family, friends, or state, or he may fall upon his knees in laughter the moment his optimism is revealed to be based upon a ghastly misreading of Proverbs 5:15. Two men of sound and healthy mind may draw upon their considerable inheritance to avoid military service, or remain in their tents with the brigade's supply of alcohol.

Men in Cars
(Previously published in *Stand*, 2019)

About war, they say, there is nothing new to disinter. It is as common to move earth with a mechanical digger, as it is to feed wild boars with the bodies of one's enemies. It is the weather on the Eastern Front, and by equal turns, the swelling over an eye, that may refresh ancient hostilities. A man engaged as an archivist at the soon-to-be-closed public library may be struggling to understand fragments of papyri, or taking notes from a maintenance manual for a Renault Megane. Two men engaged as archivists at the soon-to-be-closed public library may be jostling for the most expensive professional development opportunities, or quarrelling over a last slice of lemon meringue pie.

Men and Their Safe Places

(Previously published in *Molly Bloom*, 2018)

About war, they say, there is nothing new to upload to your Twitter feed. It is as common to keep one's erotic thoughts to oneself, as it is for them to intrude into the public sphere and cause untold consternation to your family and friends. It is the unreliable entry made about you in *A General History of the Robberies and Murders of the most notorious Pyrates*, and by equal turns, the inconvenient fact that you cannot swim, that may sell tickets to the show at Execution Dock on the Thames. A man hell-bent on getting home one day may find halfway there that his journey is essentially impossible (and a metaphor for everybody else's journey), or that when he does arrive, nobody cares and nothing seems worthy of the effort he has made. Two men hell-bent on getting home one day may find halfway there that home is now surrounded by single quote marks and appears to have become cloudy and reminiscent of dreams they used to have as teenagers, or that 'home' is the same, and it is they who have changed irreversibly.

Men More Comfortable in a Flat Back Four

(Previously published in *The Manchester Review*, 2019)

About war, they say, there is nothing new to expect from its aftermath. It is as common to come home to a performance in both song and dance of long narrative poems, as it is to come home to silence and recrimination. It is the conduct of one's heir in your absence, and by equal turns, the number of slaves one has been fortunate enough to retain in order to make a new start in the business world, that may govern which stories must be told with honesty and faithfulness, and which must be total fabrications. A man who returns from the war and becomes a notable professor of history may be disinclined to believe later revisions of a memoir because of the suspicion that they have been sexed up for reasons of political expediency, or because of the suspicion that they may have been sexed up for reasons of self-aggrandisement. Two men who return from the war and become notable professors of history may construct lucrative careers writing popular television documentaries for the Discovery Channel, or never write a single word about their experiences.

Men Manspreading on Trains

About war, they say, there is nothing new about which to alert the President. It is as common to seek regime change through force, as it is to seek it through diplomacy. It is the invasion of oil rich countries, and by equal turns, the protection of oil rich countries, that may plunge the voting public into paroxysms. A man witnessing at first hand the decisions made in the war cabinet, may be exposed as a liar by the liberal left, or accused of being a communist sympathiser by the far right. Two men witnessing at first hand the decisions made in the war cabinet may later dispute the precise language used for reasons of an accurate minute, or debate the relationship between language and reality to such a degree that they are able to assert both that nonsense and horseshit can be literally true, and that a single word can bring into existence an object that literally does not exist.

Men Raking the Long Jump Pits

About war, they say, there is nothing new to behave as an argument. It is as common to bring a present to the party, as it is to bring nothing at all. It is the truth-bearing statement that we are all going to die, and by equal turns, the truth-bearing statement that we are going to live forever, that may blow holes in one's deductive reasoning. A man who stands as the Truth Candidate for the Death Party may hope to live a very long time, or not care how long he lives as long as he lives preserving truth. Two men who stand as Truth Candidates for the Death Party may hope the voters are clever enough to see through the Live Forever Party Candidates' manifesto pledges, or be destined to cross the floor to the benches of inductive reasoning.

Men Assisted by Native Islanders

War, they say, is about nothing but business, and about both war and business, they say further, there is nothing about which to be surprised. It is as common for Hollywood to purchase the option on your novel set during the War of Jenkins's Ear, and then send it into development for twelve years before it lapses and remains unmade, as it is for a painting by Egon Schiele to be discovered under a water tank in a Viennese basement, go to auction, and be promptly stolen by hoodlums working for an unknown collector living in exile on the proceeds of unsavoury Belarusian oil deals. It is the informality of cheap transactions, and by equal turns, the regularity of knaves appearing in a hand of blackjack, that may determine who is the victor of the bragging game. A man selling his family heirlooms may be in hock to the Mob, or carrying out his solemn oath to a great aunt. Two men selling their family heirlooms may need the money to buy fabric for their standards, or playing attack against defence in the park as dusk descends.

Men with Heads for Mathematics
(Previously published in *Gutter*, 2018)

About war, they say, there is nothing new to Bcc the members of your email contact group. It is as common to focus on the evidence provided by the Food and Drugs Administration, as it is to allow a special agent to languish in an alien penal colony. It is the slaying of your mother's son, and by equal turns, the marriage to your mother's sister, that may establish you in the eyes of the populace (excluding your mother, whom you can lock up in a tower) as a man who can get things done. A man who sees war as the logical extension of foreign policy may own shares in the Lockheed Martin/Boeing F-22 Raptor, or be an academic associated with the Stockholm International Peace Research Institute whose statements are deliberately decontextualised by Fox News. Two men who see war as the logical extension of foreign policy may invoke clichéd Protestant rhetoric when faced by bereaved mothers, or be open to persuasion if a trip to Disneyland is mentioned.

Men with Tails
(Previously published in *The Moth*, 2019)

About war, they say, there is nothing new to replace with vitamin supplements. It is as common to make the tactical error of not attacking at first light, as it is to have the wizardry to attack seaward defences when nobody's looking. It is the cardboard cut-out archers in the arrow-loops, and by equal turns, the boiling syrup from the murder holes, that may inspire a man to no longer regard excessive self-concern as a failure of character. A man protecting himself from falling debris with no more than a Parisian parasol may have been caught unawares while out shopping for bread, or be a committed and faithful Looney Tunes fan. Two men protecting themselves from falling debris with no more than Parisian parasols may be suffering a peculiar form of capital punishment conceived by a certifiably mad despot, or undergoing the necessary training to become street theatre licence holders in Covent Garden.

Men in Fancy Dress
(Previously published in *International Times*, 2019)

About war, they say, there is nothing new to follow. It is as common to admire a Saxon protagonist returning home empty-handed, as it is to troll him mercilessly online. It is the buoyant nature of the bandit's manifesto, and by equal turns, the callous opportunism of his second-in-command, that may confuse the groundlings and spur them to demand their money back. A man enfeoffed with divers duchies may have collected so many titles that he decides to crown himself king of a newly-named country, or devote himself to the wishes of his many peoples. Two men enfeoffed with divers duchies may sleep unsoundly due to constant fear of invasion, or open a series of burger bars with a curiously unique selling point unrelated to either duchies or mistruths but raising instead the prospect of their customers dining with cows dressed as the Dukes of Lancaster™ (it is entirely predictable the depths to which the aristocracy will gaily plunge when faced by financial ruin).

Men Floating
(Previously published in *The Pickled Body*, 2018)

About war, they say, there is nothing new to tell the minorities. It is as common to lend money, as it is to borrow money. It is the offer of small personal loans at a high rate of interest, and by equal turns, the high risk involved in the recovery of one's investment, that may split a city in two (or even three!). A man without a licence to trade may build his illicit still deep in the woods, or give up his co-conspirators to the commissioner. Two men without a licence to trade may develop a profitable sideline in counterfeit licences, or resort to violence and intimidation.

Men in Disguise

(Previously published in *The Pickled Body*, 2018)

About war, they say, there is nothing new to take to market. It is as common to arrest the ringleaders, as it is to pardon the lot of them. It is the pace of change, and by equal turns, the irrational basis of change, that may confuse the enemy enough to steal away in the night. A man landing on a Scottish shore at the stroke of midnight may be trying to garner support for his religious delusions, or a submarine commander with a folder of top secrets. Two men landing on a Scottish shore at the stroke of midnight may provide greater international leverage than they ever imagined, or be mistaken for the tax collectors (and we know what happened to the last two bastards!).

Men with Recurring Jaundice

(Previously published in *talking about strawberries all of the time,* 2019)

About war, they say, there is nothing new to torch. It is as common to fear snow, as it is to fear bedtime. It is the photograph of the missing child carried by the mother, and by equal turns, the blood-stained pack of cigarettes found among his possessions, that may furnish us with nicknames. A man modest about himself but in love with a French soldier may apply for a job in the Seoul bureau, or throw down his hat and move onto the dancefloor. Two men modest about themselves but in love with a French soldier may draw lots, or for the first time, consider the benefits of a *ménage à trois*.

Men Hiding in the Tombs of Their Fathers

(Previously published in *Gutter*, 2018)

About war, they say, there is nothing new to confuse us. It is as common to scour the undergrowth for kindling, as it is to boil snow and grass for soup. It is the nightly airstrike, and by equal turns, the daytime shelling, that may explain the absence of a subplot. A man whose face is pressed to the window of the bus may be leaving his country forever, or finding water where he can. Two men whose faces are pressed to the window of the bus may have just resumed their friendship after thirty years of hostilities, or be going on a summer holiday.

Men Who Believe They Are Theodore Roosevelt
(Previously published in *Gutter*, 2018)

About war, they say, there is nothing new to silence us. It is as common to plan a series of five novels on the conquest of native peoples by white Europeans, as it is to complete only three and be murdered on the cathedral steps. It is the tension between tradition and modernity, and by equal turns, the cross-fertilisation of two cultures, that may have us scrabbling in the mud for the nuclear codes. A man who travels across continents to shoot a bear may be settling an old score, or have complicated relationships with women not solved by the assurance that size doesn't matter. Two men who travel across continents to shoot a bear may be members of the Boone and Crockett Club advocating the principles of the fair chase, or have complicated relationships with men not solved by the assurance that size doesn't matter.

Men Taking Capitals

About war, they say, there are no new jokes to puncture the tension. It is as common to build trade links with Marxist-Leninist one-party states, as it is to bemuse the voters of Wyoming with snake oil and general quackery. It is the pure form of reason, and by equal turns, collectively inherited patterns of thought and behaviour, that may offer your nemesis the apologias he seeks. A man clumsy and bumbling at the end of day may be a guilty signatory at the Conference of Berlin, or overcome with the joy found in imperfect copies of everything he holds dear, everything he detests, and everything he has yet to experience. Two men clumsy and bumbling at the end of the day may be on their way home from the revolution, or have lost their ball over a wall.

Men Perplexed

(Previously published in *Gutter*, 2018)

About war, they say, there is nothing new about which to be stubborn. It is as common to be called to the bar after the Restoration, as it is to watch your parents perish in a great fire. It is the machinations within the court during the dying days of a childless monarch, and by equal turns, the advice of partial councillors, that may lead the nobles to invite invasion by the King of Somewhere Else. A man found stabbed in his bed may have been controversially appointed to the Queen's privy Chamber, or have just announced his intention to run for nomination as the Republican Party's Presidential candidate. Two men found stabbed in their beds may have been messengers from the Danish court, or printers of Renaissance folios unwilling to accept that there might be more than three dramatic genres.

Men Using Pseudonyms
(Previously published in *Gutter*, 2018)

About war, they say, there is nothing new to soliloquise. It is as common to witness the decline of a once-noble hero, as it is to eat pies made of tiny tots. It is the heavy soil under which the false accusers lie, and by equal turns, the extravagant pyres on which the falsely accused burn, that may turn grief into vengeance. A man told he must die in order that morality be restored to the social world may agree with the notion that the greater good requires just such a sacrifice, or claim to be an atheist. Two men told they must die in order that morality be restored to the social world may question the latest interpretations of moral law, or suggest the identities of alternative gentlemen who could pay the ultimate price, and who can be found in plentiful number among the slums and barrios of all our cities.

Men as Unskilled Errand Boys

About war, they say, there is nothing new to condemn to labyrinths. It is as common to challenge the previous meeting's minutes, as it is to rock up to the meeting at Any Other Competent Business and complain that all the cookies are gone. It is the 13th amendment to the 13th Amendment, and by equal turns, the questionable neutrality of the inquisitors, that may induce our efforts to construct a truce to be pissed up the nearest wall. A man dividing his territories may be preparing to empower his cousins, or disenfranchise his children. Two men dividing their territories may have recognised their impending impeachments and future exile, or about to open a series of barbed wire factories to kick-start the ailing economy.

Men Making Sense of Their Feelings

About war, they say, there is nothing new to die in hospital beds. It is as common to be a small boy learning to cope with neglect, as it is to be a small boy learning to take advantage of overindulgence. It is the decision to blame women for their own small boy narcissism, and by equal turns, the decision to blame women for their own small boy excessive, self-centred, and immature anti-social behaviours, that may perpetuate a man's propensity for temper tantrums. A man unable to handle delayed gratification may take a pistol to his own brain, or masturbate furiously between the hours of 5-6 a.m. Two men unable to handle delayed gratification may join a book club for the gorging of their minds, or a rifle club for the slaking of their desires.

Men Taking Inventories

About war, they say, there is nothing new to account for it. It is as common to make a list of victories, as it is to log one's lamentations in the great book of Birth, Death & Everything in Between. It is the geography of one's moral compass, and by equal turns, the cartography of our neighbour's bigotry, that may persuade one of us to see reason. A man alphabetising his CD collection may consider himself equal in status to those granted powers of arrest, or be lost forevermore in nostalgia for albums by Birmingham's once-highly acclaimed prog-popsters, Supertramp. Two men alphabetising their CD collections may display signs of a compulsive disorder, or be wondering which of them is the greater fool: the one admired for his physicality and significant strength, or the one armed to the teeth with semi-automatic rifles.

Men on the Corner of Sunset & Vine

About war, they say, there is nothing new to prosecute for obscenity. It is as common to distribute timecoded video tapes to members of the Academy, as it is for members of the Academy to release them onto the piracy market for all and sundry to download for free. It is the damaged black and white photograph of the lemon groves, and by equal turns, the unsavoury stories from the studio backlots, that may give us the Rambo VI we deserve. A man wearing Calvin Klein underwear may do so wittingly, or unwittingly. Two men wearing Calvin Klein underwear may do so as a bet while on set for the filming of the non-CGI sequences of The Battle of Crécy, or because they are simple souls susceptible to any advertising campaign that uses Marky Mark Wahlberg as its go-to guy.

Men Doing One, Then Another

About war, they say, there is nothing left to shame us. It is as common to eat a farmer's winter crop, as it is to commandeer his daughter. It is the method of our open surrender, and by equal turns, the silence of our insurrection and the brutality of our revenge, that may fashion the consequence of our conquering. A man reading letters from home may be ashamed of his behaviour with the local barman, or ashamed of his behaviour with the local barmaid. Two men reading letters from home may be illiterate and pretending to understand the words for socio-cultural reasons, or wishing they could exchange identities and buy Far Eastern brides.

Men Naked and Alone

(Previously published in *Structo*, 2019)

About war, they say, there is nothing new to photograph. It is as common to die in old age having lived unremarkably, as it is to die young but live forever in fireside tales of gallantry and foolishness. It is the figure produced by the painstaking research of the historian, and by equal turns, the politician's denial of that figure, that may lead us to think it wasn't so bad after all. A man found in the rubble may have the scent of decaying flesh in his nostrils forevermore, or campaign for nuclear disarmament for the rest of his life. Two men found in the rubble may not recognise the city they helped to build, or know only too well the sign of man's work.

Men with Empty Fuel Tanks
(Previously published in *UCity Review*, 2020)

About war, they say, there is nothing new to enjoy. It is as common for a son to cut off his father's genitals and cast them into the sea, as it is for love to rise from that same water. It is the idea of benevolent royalty, and by equal turns, the revelation of a monarch's sexual peccadillos set out in weekly serial form for all to read and marvel at, that may, curiously, entrench the people's faith in despotism, and the people's endorsement of their own exploitation. A man able to endure suffering at the hands of a dandy may be hailed a hero, or condemned a fool. Two men able to endure suffering at the hands of a dandy may have designs upon entering high society themselves, or training for the priesthood.

Men at Funerals

(Previously published in *Structo*, 2019)

About war, they say, there is nothing new to oppose. It is as common to gather one's forces on the peninsula, as it is to send one's wife and children to a secure house. It is the bridge blown to smithereens, and by equal turns, the pilot ejecting from a burning MiG, that may make the front pages on a slow Tuesday morning. A man who says *let me walk you through this, gently* may be elderly and kind (and mortified to be told that he was being patronising), or status-hungry and completely aware of his arrogance. Two men who say *let us walk you through this, gently* may be barristers advising a client they suspect is guilty and going to be a liability on the stand, or bomb disposal experts helping you to safety.

Men Watching Girls Dance

(Previously published in *The Interpreter's House*, 2018)

About war, they say, there is nothing new to take on tour with the performing seals. It is as common to tip the mystic healer, as it is to handcuff the religious leader. It is the illegitimate orphan who grows up to be a revolutionary commander, and by equal turns, the officer who directs strategy from his room at New College while waiting to inherit his baronetcy (and whose romantic aspirations and nationalistic yearnings negate each other), that may lead to three decades of misrule. A man who begins his formal education in a single-sex environment may one day marry a young lady schooled in a single-sex environment, or remain happily unattached, as long as he has his dogs. Two men who begin their formal educations in single-sex environments may devote their lives to the political emancipation of oppressed classes in the developing world, or open a string of massage parlours in all the major port cities of Western Europe.

Men Sunbathing

(Previously published in *Structo*, 2019)

About war, they say, there is nothing new to study. It is as common for apples to be the source of all our troubles whether in ancient Greece, Norse, or Celtic (or even a garden called Eden), as it is for apples to be misinterpreted as tomatoes and cucumbers, berries and potatoes, melons and goats, oranges and nuts, jimsonweed and tree tumours, mushrooms and misogyny, and symbols of both sin and redemption. It is the fruit of perpetual sensuality, and by equal turns, the fruit that leads us to war on all fronts, that may tie us to trees to face the crossbow. A man wassailing through the orchards of Somerset may want no more than to bless the trees and wish for a bumper crop of cider apples, or he may want to bang pots and pans as hard as he can, and fire his gun into the night to drive away his demons. Two men wassailing through the orchards of Somerset may be farmers from Devon intent upon sabotage, or Jed and Bazzer who come every year because they fancy Alwyn the Wassail Queen, and have spent many an hour discussing how they would show their affection for her if only she would let them.

Men Who Write Sequels

(Previously published in *Five:2:One*, 2019)

About war, they say, there is nothing new to hold one's parents responsible for. It is as common to have one's novel about the gradual loss of a way of life to be gradually forgotten and all remaining copies pulped, as it is to have it adapted for the stage as a successful, if controversial, musical. It is the peaceful secession from the union, and by equal turns, the carnage that ensues, that may lead us once more to long for the hurly-burly of that belittled, disparaged, and vilified union. A man who turns to his lover in the cold half-light of dawn and says *I fear being insubstantial* may also yearn to be mentioned obliquely in a short story about something far more important than he can ever be, or he may wish that he was substantial enough for his lover to be awake to hear this weak supplication and offer somehow to allay his fear. Two men who turn to their lover in the cold half-light of dawn and say *We fear being insubstantial* may wonder why they are sleeping in the same room as each other's lover (it's because they have both forgotten the pact they made), or they may finally admit they are each other's lover and that this revelation means they no longer need to prove themselves substantial on the battlefield.

Men in Slow Motion
(Previously published in *UCity Review*, 2020)

About war, they say, there is nothing new to entrance us. It is as common to adopt an eagle for its grace and intuition, as it is to climb to its eyrie and smash its chick to death. It is the search for the bodies, and by equal turns, the unknown coordinates of the crash site, that may cause the Canadian bombardiers browsing the shelves of the *boucherie* to name their pet kittens Pride and Prejudice, and then forget which is which. A man baffled and aghast at the wreckage to his home may be so enervated he may never lift another book, or so energised he immediately runs to the ruins of his library to take up his pen and invent new forms of expression. Two men baffled and aghast at the wreckage of their homes may mobilise their neighbours to rampage through the streets outside the town hall, or join a group of botanists on an expedition to the fragile grasslands of Central Asia with the express purpose of clarifying the confusing issues whipped up by earlier botanical research carried out by plant ecologists who work across town in a rival university.

Men Strolling Through Lavender
(Previously published in *UCity Review*, 2020)

About war, they say, there is nothing new to influence the military-industrial complex. It is as common to believe conflict has no beginning, as it is to believe it has no end. It is the enormity of defence spending, and by equal turns, the peaceful nature of its goal, that may send a man to fight in the desert with a faulty rocket launcher. A man who marries in secret may do so because his spouse prefers it that way, or because both he and his spouse will be subjected to the vilification normally reserved for cut-throats and blackguards. Two men who marry in secret may be part of a cult planning their escape, or, confusingly, the man and his spouse mentioned earlier.

Men Undergoing Surgery
(Previously published in *Denver Quarterly*, 2020)

The war wants men to report it. It is as common to wire in one's despatch from a brothel in Las Vegas while claiming to be on the Syrian front, as it is to retreat into the Andes for three months in order to protect a source. It is the infectious diseases, and by equal turns, the violent deaths of priests, that may shape our names for good or bad. A man claiming to be ignorant of the war's function and aspirations may be appealing to his electoral base, or hoping for a slice of lemon tart from the trolley reserved for first class passengers. Two men claiming to be ignorant of the war's function and aspirations may be planning their spring break in Fort Lauderdale, or stockpiling rifles and grenades in a quiet suburb.

Men with Lattes

(Previously published in *Anthropocene*, 2019)

About war, they say, there is nothing new to download. It is as common to be overwhelmed by choice, as it is to rage against its perceived scarcity. It is the romance of long summers passed away in garden parties, and by equal turns, the polar bear drifting to its doom on a wafer of ice, that may jab us in the eye with blackthorn. A man who puts down his horse without the aid of chemicals may have been disciplined in this art during his tours of duty, or be extremely disoriented by hunger and the alien environment. Two men who put down their horses without the aid of chemicals may have no choice due to the barbarities of the battlefield, or be inside an allegory wrought by an author ill-disposed to the objections of effete aristocrats.

Men Hours from Victory

(Previously published in *The Manchester Review*, 2019)

About war, they say, there is nothing new to refute. It is as common to drain a swamp, as it is to redirect it. It is the child's fib concerning the broken saucer, and by equal turns, the bald man's poorly fitting wig, that may create the holes into which we can throw our virtues. A man who claims to be a bear may exhibit bear-like behaviours but still not be a bear (despite his protestations), or he may have enough money to persuade squirrels, mice, deer, and sundry other wildlife that they too are bears. Two men who claim to be bears may be so frightening that nobody dares to tell them they are not bears, or have once been on the roster at Soldier Field and therefore, technically, they are indeed bears (and bears who drink beer, no less).

Men with Too Much Time to Think

(Previously published in *The Poets' Republic*, 2018)

About war, they say, there is nothing new to understand. It is as common to be comforted by giants, as it is to be spooked by pixies. It is the return of lost brothers, and by equal turns, the betrayal by trusted manservants, that may move us to sell our land to the first buyer who offers a reasonable price. A man who lives in a terraced house in north London may be the blind seer foretold, or a ruthless landlord exploiting the poor with the aid of financial inducements ratified by both local and national government. Two men who live in a terraced house in north London may find their love stretched to breaking twice a year when Spurs play Arsenal, or be trying to learn enough English to get themselves jobs.

Men Writing Wills

(Previously published in *Molly Bloom*, 2018)

About war, they say, there is nothing new to place on a plinth. It is as common to spend the nation's taxes on gambling and cigars, as it is to replace its rookeries with social housing. It is the man unencumbered by responsibilities, and by equal turns, the man radicalised by Puritanism, that may establish a man's legacy as either intact or in tatters. A man hired to inscribe the capital's triumphal arches with the names of victorious battles may be fired for wilful misspellings, or begin to subcontract the work to immigrants at depressed hourly rates so that he may spend more time at the greyhounds. Two men hired to inscribe the capital's triumphal arches with the names of victorious battles may never become bored by the malleability of limestone, or start their work at either end planning to meet in the middle but die of old age before the plan's fruition.

Men with Spare Tyres
(Previously published in *Molly Bloom*, 2018)

About war, they say, there is nothing new to outsource. It is as common to grow weary of protecting one's self, as it is to be hired to protect others. It is the faith in a beautiful hereafter, and by equal turns, the carnal delights of the here-and-now, that may reduce a man's army to pusillanimity. A man realising too late that he has become defenceless prey to the barbarians may ally himself with those very barbarians, or found a new religious sect preaching servility and mollification. Two men realising too late that they have become defenceless prey to the barbarians may tour the bars of the old harbour in search of malcontents to raise a newly modelled army, or destroy the tanks, lay the mines, and burn the wells as they withdraw.

Men in Big Coats

(Previously published in Molly Bloom, 2018)

About war, they say, there is nothing new to offer the Russians. It is as common to erect monoliths across the vanquished homelands, each with increasing opulence, as it is to issue anti-monolith samizdat in the cafes, parks, and bars. It is thc sccret police sent to unearth the undercover resistance, and by equal turns, the unexpected rise of feminism, that may inspire foreboding and despondence on Air Force One. A man who writes of his need to play a gallant role in the war may die of lunacy, or contagion. Two men who write of their need to play a gallant role in the war may return home to Oxford to complete their studies, or quickly tire of civilian life and become mercenaries, forever searching for that perfect hit.

Men Adapting Short Stories
(Previously published in Glasgow Review of Books, 2018)

About war, they say, there is nothing new to ready us for death. It is as common to peer through the branches at a man about to be hanged, as it is to question our suspension of civilian morality. It is the sentimental attachment to our country and our family, and by equal turns, the delusion that something noble lies at the heart of our white-knuckle endeavours, that may destroy our urge for a happy ending. A man surfacing from the depths of a river may stumble through the birch to find his lover, or disrupt the narrative to no political end. Two men surfacing from the depths of a river may convince themselves their cause is just so they may brutalise non-combatants, or hand in their comrades to save their own necks.

Men Dubious of Collective Goals

(Previously published in *Hypnopomp*, 2018)

About war, they say, there is nothing new to hide in the hotel's lobby. It is as common to find the city looks the same as it did on your previous visit, as it is to wonder if you have come upon the village of perpetual change as foretold in the ancient prophesies. It is the inability to sleep, and by equal turns, the inability to speak, that may determine whether one ever regains a foothold in contemporary society. A man found dead on the banks of a river may be left to rot in the sun, or rolled into the water by otters. Two men found dead on the banks of a river may be kept alive in the stories told of them by friends and strangers, or be forgotten forever.

Men and Their Children

(Previously published in *Glasgow Review of Books*, 2018)

About war, they say, there is nothing new to reflect. It is as common to peer into glassy water and die of self-love, as it is to smash mirrors on the tiled floor and dance in its bloody chaos. It is the knowledge one acquires by others' perception of you, and by equal turns, the ignorance one hoards in denying one's perception by others, that may lead a single man to force his countrymen and his enemies onto the wild moors. A man with $11 million to spend may find himself bankrupt within minutes of landing in Las Vegas, or about to realise his magnum opus. Two men with $11 million to spend may feel they can afford not to forgive their treacherous offspring despite the entreaties of their fool, or buy themselves a French second division striker for their latest push for promotion.

Men Gone AWOL

About war, they say, there is nothing left on which to base our movies. It is as common to watch a Russian double–agent played by an English public schoolboy, as it is to gain entrance to the Asian-themed cabaret club 'Forbidden City' at 363 Sutter Street, San Francisco, on a busy Saturday night in 1940 *('Come Early! Dinner 5:30 Dancing 6:30 First Show 7.30')* – as long as you have the requisite capital. You may confront your past like a soldier, or you may confront your past like an academic. Either way, you can't touch the girls. (They'll be back tomorrow.) A man on a roof making a celebrated speech in the rain may be hatching a desperate plan to debunk the very foundations of social psychology, or acutely anxious about the indistinct mark set by a grumpy cinematographer. Two men on a roof making a celebrated speech in the rain may be completing a chaotic rehearsal for a PhD viva, or estate agents discussing their disappointments while having a cigarette break.

Men Passing Beggars

About war, they say, there is nothing new to prolong one's lunch break. It is as common to buy your colleague the wrong sandwich, as it is to go hungry for charitable purposes. It is the gift without expectation of reciprocity, and by equal turns, the lack of empathy shown to others without clear medical grounds as excuse, that may close the market early and return us empty-handed to our families. A man who admits to personal gratification from the pleasure of others may be undivided on the competing ethical doctrines of Those on The Left and Those on The Right, or in dire need of a good night out with the lads. Two men who admit to personal gratification from the pleasure of others may be open source software developers whose only motive is the free dissemination of knowledge, or hackers intent on the destruction of Western democratic elections.

Men as Palimpsests

About war, they say, there is nothing new to reveal. It is as common to begin a story on a country road, as it is to end it on a country road (often the same road) (but in a different direction). It is the city built in the flatlands, and by equal turns, the city built on the city in the flatlands, that may point us toward a tower of cities built in the flatlands, thus making them no more a vast realm of flatlands but a man-made mountain of concrete and steel. A man born in the bottom city may be revered as a founding father, or treated like a dog with the mange. Two men born in the bottom city may scratch and grind until they reach the top city (and at which point play the parlour game Last Man Standing), or be content to view the many cities as one city.

Men with Wooden Legs
(Previously published in *talking about strawberries all of the time*, 2019)

About war, they say, there is nothing new to medicate. It is as common to bombard your enemy's weakest link, as it is to seize your enemy's fleet to secure the shipping lanes. It is the denial of access to the raw materials for building roads, houses, ships, and tea strainers, and by equal turns, the rumours of a long, grim, and vote-losing blockade, that may lead us to reintroduce conscription. A man given 700 lashes may be a deserter, or an excessively fervent door-to-door salesman who won't take no for an answer. Two men given 700 lashes may have organised bare-knuckle fights in the Junior Ranks' Mess, or been found guilty of 'looking at the sky'.

Men in Rome

(Previously published in Glasgow Review of Books, 2018)

About war, they say, there is nothing new to defend. It is as common to respect a city's capitulation, as it is to bomb the place to hell. It is the old jokes that never die, and by equal turns, the perennial tyrannies returning each spring, that may fill an atheist with a soul in which he doesn't believe. A man who shoots a pregnant woman in the back may have his finger on the trigger, or the camera. Two men who shoot a pregnant woman in the back may do it for the glory of the fatherland, or for a line of coke and a fur coat.

Men Wearing Thorns
(Previously published in *Hypnopomp*, 2018)

About war, they say, there is nothing new to put us in a blue funk. It is as common to feel pain, as it is to feel fear. It is the mistake made by your enemy to think that pain will make you confess, and by equal turns, the mistake made by your comrades to think that your physical wounds put them in peril, that may place you in a dock praying your loved ones will not lie to protect you. A man may live with pain; a man may say *You cannot hurt me,* and it may be true. Two men may live with pain; two men may say *Pain will never defeat us. It's our fear that will defeat us,* and this too, may be true.

Men Talking to Crows

About war, they say, there is nothing new to mar the shadows. It is as common to praise Babylon for its architecture, as it is to impute Persepolis for its secularism. It is the rampant ague, and by equal turns, the unbridled illiteracy, that may lose a man his pension. A man deemed unfit to rule may try to bend the ear of the monarch's trusted advisor, or have his doctors beaten. Two men deemed unfit to rule may throw their young under a bus, or have their doctors paid handsomely to reverse their diagnoses.

Men Who Win at Trivial Pursuits

The history of cities is the history of sitting in cafes documenting experience. Murder may be a simple means of collecting insurance. Palimpsests may sound like a very solid form of making (though we all know this to be untrue) (or at least questionable). All histories make the shape of a man's anger into its own mirror image. This dampens the sound and later echo of conflict. A half-assembled history feels better on the skin than one found inside itself, where the elements of sun, rain, and wind lead to inevitable erosions. In these circumstances, a man's dilemma, in the strained stillness of night, may be to permit these extinctions, or oppose them.

Men Hunting New Moons
(Previously published in *UCity Review*, 2020)

About war, they say, there is nothing new to edit. It is as common to marry the last G.I. to leave the country, as it is to divorce him as soon as you set foot on dry land. It is the dawn that resembles your homeland, and by equal turns, the dusk that resembles the moment of your family's slaughter, that may lead us all into temptation. A man riding the fin of a bottlenose dolphin may be a happy-go-lucky surfer, or an Etruscan pirate in the process of transformation at the hands of a compassionate Dionysus. Two men riding the fins of bottlenose dolphins may be stirred by the prospect of sea pig cubes fried in miso sauce with vegetables, or rogue elements of the U.S. Navy Marine Mammal Program training dolphins to attack and kill deep sea divers.

Men Who Wish for Single Pantheons

About war, they say, there is nothing new to translate. It is as common to build a city of scholarly debate, as it is to dredge the canals for discarded discourse. It is the fragments we use to construct our accounts of the conflict, and by equal turns, the redactions we license, that may be collected by our children in the future and used as evidence against us. A man weighing the surviving sources as if they were mouldy onions may be no man at all, or a man put in charge of the library's empty wing. Two men weighing the surviving sources as if they were mouldy onions may be travellers with spears and spells to cast, or utterly confused passengers from the cruise ship who seek the harbour but are unable to converse with the locals as sailing time approaches.

Men and Poppies

About war, they say, there is nothing new to pioneer. It is as common to cross the Equator by palanquin, as it is to slaughter the great American bison. It is the bacteria in the blankets, and by equal turns, the remedies of the local healers, that may cause us to wage a pitiless campaign of abuse against the donut store management. A man watching his fellow passengers sleep may be driven to reconsider the blame he attaches to his failed relationships with women, or giddy with the drunkenness of high-speed travel. Two men watching their fellow passengers sleep may be bracing themselves for inspection at the border, or wondering into which carriage the rest of their team mates have gone, indeed, whether their team mates alighted at an earlier station and left them to travel alone.

Men Beasting It

(Previously published in *Palaver*, 2021)

About war, they say, there is nothing new to discuss at the gym. It is as common to dip, as it is to spin. It is the size of the protein window, and by equal turns, the unnaturally fast heartbeat, that may make us run for the door without showering. A man who says *you being insecure doesn't make me elitist – that's not how logic works* may have liver damage and peeling skin, or be an inspector from the Foods Standards Agency. Two men who say *you being insecure doesn't make us elitist – that's not how logic works* may meet in pubs each month to deconstruct the lyric of 'Wichita Lineman', or be the research assistants of newly-elected parliamentarians hatching a plan to infiltrate the government with nasty little fascists who got bullied at school.

Men Educating Princes
(Previously published in *PoetryBirmingham*, 2019)

About war, they say, there is nothing new to drive us mad. It is as common to seek motive in the text, as it is to discover motive in the green room. It is the body in the lake, and by equal turns, the potion in the glass, that may confound the women once more. A man laying down his lance for a room full of books may be haunted by the ghosts of his former lovers, or banished to Lusitania. Two men laying down their lances for a roomful of books may soon realise that silence contains its own peculiar form of danger, or be ready, finally, to read Seneca by candlelight.

Men Who Own Screwdrivers
(Previously published in *Poetry Birmingham*, 2019)

Men admire each other's martial arts, particularly during periods of severe economic crises. A dire strait filled with water may be as easily circumnavigated as a dire strait made of jam and holes, but a comma mistaken for a semi-colon may stop up the dam forever and a day. If war is a distinguishing characteristic of human nature, how might we explain the existence of music? If war is a controlled over-reaction to poverty and hurricanes, how might we resist big old men and their annihilations? Men sit down to discuss these matters over dinner with cocaine and strippers. Men may need our help.

Men, Unclassified

About war, they say, there is nothing new to make us reconsider our priorities. It is as common to leave our comrades lying in no man's land, as it is to risk our lives to bury them respectfully. It is the decision to obey your god, and by equal turns, the decision to follow your leader, that may lead us all to a long and lonely end. A man who gradually assimilates into local culture and disappears into the jungle may draw the wrath and search parties of the empire's army, or prosper and die of joy and syphilis. Two men who gradually assimilate into local culture and disappear into the jungle may train rebels in new forms of guerrilla tactics, or emerge thirty years later to a thunderous media storm from which they never escape.

Men Who Prefer Dogs

About war, they say, there is nothing new to compose. It is as common to surrender at the sight of the royal hounds, as it is to climb the ancient oak for safety. It is the sensation of sharp steel at one's throat, and by equal turns, the feel of the conductor's baton as it brushes the back of your hand, that may remind of us of that night in the Sydney Opera House when they played 'Cavatina'. A man whose father served in the Middle East may keep his dog tags in a drawer under his clean socks, or wear them around his neck on special occasions. Two men whose fathers served in the Middle East may one day want to emulate their heroic deeds and sad deaths, or march down The Strand against the senselessness of war and get arrested for affray.

Men at Boarding School

About war, they say, there is nothing new to segregate the children. It is as common to embrace the House system, as it is to weep softly into one's pillow at lights out in the dorm. It is the healthy rivalry, and by equal turns, the bouts of violence, depression, and xenophobia, that may groom men to become your political & big business leaders. A man bullied into doing a prefect's homework may one day become the CEO who handles all your water and environmental needs, or write opinion pieces for a national daily newspaper. Two men bullied into doing a prefect's homework may become 21st century equivalents to Leopold and Loeb, or Laurel and Hardy; either way, they'll be the next Prime Minister and Chancellor of the Exchequer.

Men Who Meet Shepherds

About war, they say, there is nothing new to choreograph. It is as common for the villagers to hide you from the rebels in a wall cavity, as it is for them to drown you in a well. It is the box ticked erroneously in the report, and by equal turns, the misread radio signal, that may guide the Resistance straight to your door. A man giving the benefit of the doubt to a handful of backpackers bearing little but torn shirts, Phrygian caps, and body lice may offer them a lift to the next town, or pop into Greggs for a bag of sausage rolls. Two men giving the benefit of the doubt to a handful of backpackers bearing little but torn shirts, Phrygian caps, and body lice may wish they had studied harder at school so that they knew what 'alms' were (and where they might be able to purchase some), or snatch the opportunity to lead those less fortunate than themselves in a short prayer in order to bask in the narcissistic glow of moral grandstanding.

Men on Long Drives

(Previously published in *The Manchester Review*, 2019)

About war, they say, there is nothing new to drop thoughtlessly in the gutter. It is as common to cry at your mother's deathbed, as it is to evict her from the family home and trash her collection of worthless china. It is the grand hall made of gold and ebony, and by equal turns, the house made from twigs and hair, that may invite us to see in the New Year (for reasons of networking – expect to leave early). A man who hides his car and turns out all the lights to avoid his neighbour's party may have designs upon a quiet night in with his laptop, or be slightly morose at this time of year and too kind to subject his mild depression on others. Two men who hide their cars and turn out their lights to avoid their neighbour's party may be no longer speaking to their neighbour because of the incident with the cricket balls at the previous party, or have forgotten what day it is.

Men as Contestants
(Previously published in *Five:2:One*, 2019)

About war, they say, there is nothing new to win. It is as common to choose the microwave oven over the baroque glassware, as it is to throw hoops around all twenty-five plastic dinosaurs. It is the dwindling inheritance, and by equal turns, the windfall from a stolen lottery ticket, that may stake one's claim to be the rightful Duke of Bologna. A man appalled by the fascist-era facades of his native city may flee to the port of Bristol seeking passage to the New World, or begin a short-lived affair with a ship's cook. Two men appalled by the fascist-era facades of their native city may play paper-rock-scissors for the cuddly toy at the end of the conveyor belt, or disagree over the latest *cause célèbre* of the London stage, one believing the 'thumb defence', the other believing the 'actual penis' allegation.

Men Awaiting Assignments

(Previously published in *The Fortnightly Review*, 2020)

About war, they say, there is nothing new to cannibalise. It is as common to celebrate intelligence, as it is to be entertained by stupidity. It is the widespread regard for monsters, and by equal turns, the widespread fear of monsters, that may reduce our susceptibility to notions of 'monsters'. A man bold and conceptual in his use of language may disregard all reviews (particularly those in *The Edinburgh Review*), or grow discontent with the product of his practice. Two men bold and conceptual in their use of language may change agent after every project, or attempt to pare language down to their static floor shows, such that we begin to read their bodies as violence committed in silent and motionless space.

Men on Rooftops
(Previously published in *Palaver*, 2021)

About war, they say, there is nothing new at which to point one's finger. It is as common to break the terms of a treaty, as it is to argue over the meaning of a treaty. It is the unsent telegram, and by equal turns, the arrival of the mysterious letter, that may knock heads together and bring the participants to the table of a third party. A man who claims to have not slaughtered civilians but encouraged them to fight alongside him may have enough photographic evidence to exonerate himself, or he may have no other recourse but to repeat his spurious claim over and over until he is taken outside and shot by the authorities. Two men who claim to have not slaughtered civilians but encouraged them to fight alongside them may have read this defence in an account of the Sino-Soviet conflict of 1929 while Humanities undergraduates at the University of Essex, or a pair of cowardy-cowardy custards unfit for military leadership roles.

Men Departing from Classical Models
(Previously published in *Rise Up Review*, 2020)

About war, they say, there is nothing new to walk behind. It is as common to be exiled to the Levant, as it is to plant one's feet in the soil of one's ancestors and feel their fingers stroke your soles. It is the belief that allowing women the vote may lead them into lesbianism, prostitution, necrophilia, gambling, driving cars, and all manner of licentiousness, and by equal turns, that the re-nationalisation of the railways may be the first step toward the death of all that is holy, that may enrage the Prince Consort and his Prime Minister. A man who needs his war to fill his belly may reluctantly take in lodgers in bad times, or open a café near the beach selling weak tea and cheap digestive biscuits bought from an out of town cash-and-carry. Two men who need their wars to fill their bellies may exhibit signs of gaiety in the trenches, or put the gouging of Gloucester's eyes on a YouTube loop to repeat at their leisure. (You can support YouTubeLoop.net by making a monetary donation.)

Men Without Surnames

About war, they say, there is nothing new to make us feel tingly in the night. It is as common to anglicise one's name for ease of pronunciation, as it is to adopt one's ancient Gaelic name to redress a few imbalances. It is the lack of clean laundry, and by equal turns, the preponderance of wild dogs prowling the city streets, that may persuade the pilots to take their R&R at any one of the many hot springs scattered around the islands. A man juggling chainsaws may have found a Roundhead in his bed, or a Cavalier in his bathroom. Two men juggling chainsaws may have made a pact to spend the winter in Paris hiding from the Prussians (BAD decision![1]), or be practising one-handed for a second and final attempt at the world record for juggling chainsaws[2] (slightly less BAD decision!).

[1] (it is a well-known fact that it is impossible to hide from the Prussians)

[2] (presently 94 in 37 seconds using 3 fully engaged chainsaws)

Men Bunking Off

About war, they say, there is nothing new to footnote. It is as common to prophesise a final battle of the end times, as it is to snigger at the loonies. It is the proliferation of white horses, and by equal turns, the suspicion triggered by contradictions inherent in various 'end' times being followed by 're-births' and 'renewals', that may give us pause to consider whether any of this shit makes the slightest bit of sense. A man who can think of nothing worse than all the dead rising on the Day of Judgment may refute the idea that his racist father is a racist (thus revealing himself to be a racist), or merely be anxious that Jerry Davies from Year 9 who died in a road traffic accident when he was twenty-two will come back to bully him like he did in the playground of St Saviour's Primary School. Two men who can think of nothing worse than all the dead rising on the Day of Judgment may be worried that every single one of them will be an Arsenal supporter, or convinced it will be the same old same old as far as who gets rewarded and who gets punished.

Men Denied Access to the Poop Deck
(Previously published in *Hypnopomp*, 2018)

About war, they say, there is nothing new to tell Lucille. It is as common for a Lieutenant-Admiral to have his portrait painted wearing pyjamas and chocolate coins, as it is for him to sling a red curtain over his shoulders and place a hand on his hip. It is the convoy escorting merchant ships through the Channel, and by equal turns, the favourable wind, that may guide the fleet into safe harbour and a final night in the brothels of Lowestoft. A man accused of being a member of the intelligentsia may have his head struck from his body on the banks of the Rhine, or hanged in the prison grounds of Kentucky. Two men accused of being members of the intelligentsia may be killed in the shelling of a highly populated civilian area, namely a public park, as a result of the indiscriminate use of truck-mounted multiple rocket launchers, or throw away their dictionaries and learn how to plaster walls.

Men in Spotlights

About war, they say, there is nothing to resurface with vigour and fertility after the inevitable floods. It is as common to be kidnapped by faeries, as it is to be turned into beasts of ambiguous sexualities. It is the loneliness, and by cqual turns, the inability to communicate, that may feed us with the hysterical strength of twenty men. A man who lives in a caravan park may be able to quote Erasmus on the evils of warfare, or be very short of money. Two men who live in a caravan park may be collaborating on a manual deriding the 16th century retention of the longbow, or legionnaires lying low for the winter.

Men Rising Early

About war, they say, there is nothing new to release straight to cheap subscription streaming services. It is as common to bicker over minor translations as it is to reinterpret an entire oeuvre to mean the opposite of its original reading and cause a string of neighbouring nations to descend into a hundred years of border warfare. It is the retreat to Virginia, and by equal turns, the advance on Moscow, that may trap us on a narrow bridge near Stirling. A man pinned down in the western theatre without provisions may decide to advance despite his numerical inferiority, or nip out during the intermission for popcorn and cola. Two men pinned down in the western theatre may capitulate and throw themselves on the mercy of their enemies, or sell their uniforms to the rebels and see out their lives farming the Highveld.

Men Who Chain Their Dogs

About war, they say, there is nothing new to survive. It is as common to tamper with your gods to make them fit snugly into the new fashion, as it is to stay well clear of divinities and their wackadoodle disciples. It is the fields sown with fire, and by equal turns, the stars turned to vapour, that may whip up belief in dragons. A man who throws off his armour may take up the saxophone and tour Eastern Europe with his newly-formed jazz quintet, or open a pub next door to a railway station. Two men who throw off their armour may do so because their masters have tired of combat, or because the rust is irritating their skin.

Men in Speedboats
(Previously published in *Drunk Monkeys*, 2019)

About war, they say, there is nothing new to support. It is as common to wear braces to hold up one's pants, as it is to wear one's pants outside one's trousers. It is the magician in the parlour, and by equal turns, the magician's assistant left outside in the rain, that may make us reconsider our investment in the sandalwood harvest. A man partial to cigars whatever the weather may be heading to the cove where the shipwreck was reported, or fixing a pipe to the exhaust. Two men partial to cigars whatever the weather may be opium smugglers bartering for a sack of shot, or Edwardian diarists wondering if the unremitting sun will ever set again.

Men Confused by Assassinations

About war, they say, there is nothing new to uncover with polygraphs. It is as common to desire one's own rescue, as it is to avoid detection at all costs. It is the wearing of purple robes and body armour in maths classes, and by equal turns, the recently introduced policy document forbidding the failure of tests, that may raise a nation's education system into the Top Ten of Something Or Other. A man on a roof with a rifle and bar of chocolate may be a rebel sniper having second thoughts, or a fan of the Marvel comic series looking for peace and quiet. Two men on a roof with rifles and bars of chocolate may take the consequences of their probable martyrdom extremely seriously, or each be plotting the other's murder to conceal their own duplicitous collaboration with the enemy.

Men Passing the Buck

(Previously published in *Denver Quarterly*, 2020)

About war, they say, there is nothing new to deport. It is as common to support the extradition of all civilian refugees, as it is to offer them sanctuary in the tabernacle. It is the place of origin, and by equal turns, the ultimate destination, that may provide the authorities with the justification they seek to abandon us. A man fleeing the countryside because the harvest failed may become a bright young thing in the city, or starve to death on its pavements. Two men fleeing the countryside because the harvest failed may not be believed because officially the harvest hasn't failed and to say it has is illegal, or they may join the underground newspaper and face the ceaseless prospect of capture.

Men Facing Significant Disruption

(Previously published in *Foxtrot Uniform*, 2019)

About war, they say, there is nothing new to abandon in a state of awkward and dishevelled eroticism. It is as common to place one's copy of War for Boys prominently in one's bookshelf, as it is to scrawl rude and childish line drawings in its margins. It is the graphic nature of the violent set pieces, and by equal turns, the nebulous attachment to historical truth, that may help the movie version of the book to overcome its entirely negative reviews and turn a substantial profit. A man who wields a long sword in each hand simultaneously may be better prepared to meet several adversaries at once, or too knackered to fight at all. Two men wielding long swords in each hand simultaneously may be devoted guards protecting the Royal Academy, or have just been told that all trains from London Euston to East Croydon via Thornton Heath have been cancelled for the next four hours.

Men Who Believe Themselves

(Previously published in *Shearsman*, 2018)

Men in twos may be lining up for more *salade Niçoise*, or apologising for all the pyromania. A man crying while at the same time laughing may be having trouble composing himself, or dreaming of his days strutting the boards of the South Bank in an all-nude production of Antony and Cleopatra. It is the level of stock in the munitions factory, and by equal turns, the classical structure of a burning city viewed from a far hilltop, that may translate self-pity into wonder. It is the unexceptional. It is the heavily built mundanity. It is the plain-vanilla voracity. About war, they say, there is nothing left to believe.

Men at the Pub Quiz

(Previously published in *The Fortnightly Review*, 2020)

About war, they say, there is nothing new to do when living near the Equator. It is as common to repel the east and west, as it is the north and south. It is the slapped face of Alexander, and by equal turns, the kicked arse of Genghis Khan, that may steel a man's backbone when the British and Russians come calling. A man skilled at playing the Buffer Game may be fluent in thirteen languages, or deficient in all but his own. Two men skilled at playing the Buffer Game may be blackmailed into espionage, or astonished that somebody once considered inventing a game from which nobody emerges as victor.

Men as Architects

(Previously published in *The Fortnightly Review*, 2020)

About war, they say, there is nothing new to plan, design, and execute. It is as common to be mightily addicted to rum, as it is to crave the company of unknown spectators at the carnival. It is the driving out of evil night spirits, and by equal turns, the welcoming of longer days and unrestrained fertility, that may excuse a whole community their neglect of the poor and their burning of witches. A man who builds cities may use bricks, or he may use stories. Two men who build cities may view them from the safety of their drawings alone, or as a pair of spunky *flâneurs* knowing the cities will crumble with or without their assistance, and with or without an army at their walls.

Men Who Believe Themselves of Noble Birth

About war, they say, there is nothing new for which to feel contempt. It is as common to lose one's faith, as it is to adopt the cause of one nation under a god, indivisible, facing nothing but a glorious future. It is the weight of the snow on your windscreen, and by equal turns, one's interpretation of the street signs pointing toward the great city on the plain, that may determine to which hospital you may be taken in order to recuperate with, or without, the desecration of your limbs. A man who believes himself to be an expert in metallurgy may switch his interest and professional efforts to robbery and murder on the merest whim, or inculcate a passion for anti-intellectualism in his children. Two men who believe themselves to be experts in metallurgy may hover between acts of timid servility and acts of barbarism, or hang out with scientists until the statute of limitations expires.

Men Who Believe Themselves Caricatures
(Previously published in *Shearsman*, 2018)

About war, they say, there is nothing new to describe.

And yet they do. As often as they imitate their fathers.

As frequently as they exaggerate their masculine features.

Even as they are revealed to be of 'least concern' to international conservation experts.

A man may be compared to a hairy woodpecker, or take offence to an ill-judged emoji. Two men compared to hairy woodpeckers are unlikely to be hairy woodpeckers, despite the protestations of literal minded zealots.

Men Who Buy Gifts
(Previously published in *talking strawberries all of the time*, 2019)

Capitalism is a disease, they say. Every so often, it must lance its boils with a small dose of fascism. At these times, a man may pray the inevitable puss of war squirts into somebody else's country, or be willing to take up arms himself. At these times, two men praying just make things worse.

Men, As a Matter of Fact
(Previously published in *New Writing Scotland 37*, 2019)

About war, they say, there is nothing new to serve with a first-class mayonnaise. It is as common to prohibit the production, conveyance, and sale of popular novels, as it is to ban the use of cars and public transport to those in low-income families. Which is to say, not very common. But it is common for men to hanker after the legitimisation of these options. Especially the one with the novels. Men would very much like to ban novels, and moreover, to take aside their authors and throw them from clifftops into the ravine. *Men who write novels cannot be trusted*, they say. *In fact, plays and poems are just as bad. Though art never built a railway, or ploughed a field, artists are dangerous. We need more clifftops*, they say. It is the ability to complete and file one's own tax return, and by equal turns, the widespread availability of blank till receipts, that may upskill the work force. A man granted the authority and leave to hold weekly markets in the town square may demand two such days be tax free (specifically the feast days of St Augustine of Hippo, and St Basil Fool for Christ), or extract inflated fees with menaces because he doesn't give a shit about maintaining important social ties between urban and rural communities. Two men granted the authority and leave to hold weekly markets in the town square may happily collect all the booth fees themselves, or ask for a hint as to the true identity of he who wanders the market in long black cloak and hood and to whom all the market stall holders give freely of their goods and services. He who wears the long black cloak and hood is not a ghost, but he haunts the men's thoughts and feelings, to the point whereby they can no longer enjoy their weekly markets, nor the vast sums of money they earn from them.

Men Recalibrate Their Sights

About war, they say, there is nothing new to resurrect. It is as common to disregard defeat, as it is to be disgruntled by success. It is a faith in extreme methods of population control, and by equal turns, a faith in faith as an easy justification of one's continued belligerence, that may pay the infantrymen's wages. A man unqualified to lead but skilled at the interview process may surely receive a position beyond his capacities, but never the respect of his subordinates. Not that he will care. He is a hound in pursuit of a kitten, a spineless git in pursuit of mastery. Two men unqualified to lead but skilled at the interview process may know and exploit to their advantage the difference between negotiation and consultation, leadership and management, hawks and doves, competence and incompetence, skill and buffoonery. They are dogged in their pursuit of the trump cards. Men are relentless.

About the Author

Mark Russell's previous full collections are Shopping for Punks (*Hesterglock*, 2017), and Spearmint & Rescue (*Pindrop*, 2016). His full collection Come to the River (*Beir Bua*), is due to be published in early 2023. He has published five pamphlets/ chapbooks: (the book of gatherings) (*Red Ceilings*, 2020); (the book of moose) (*Kattywompus*, USA, 2016); (the book of seals) (*Red Ceilings*, 2016); Saturday Morning Pictures (*Red Ceilings*, 2015), and Pursued by Well-being (*tall-lighthouse*, 2013).

Mark studied in Liverpool where he gained a first in Drama & English, and then won a British Academy award to take a Masters in Theatre Studies at Leeds. Before moving to Scotland, he worked as a lecturer in Theatre Arts at Addis Ababa University, and as a journalist in Cornwall.

During his career as a teacher of Drama, Mark has written educational books and materials for theatre productions, and on several subjects including Contemporary Scottish Theatre, Brecht, Artaud, Shakespeare, Tennessee Williams, and Augusto Boal.

His plays have been performed at the Glasgow West End Festival, in Edinburgh, as a rehearsed reading at the Citizens' Theatre by the Playwrights' Studio, Scotland, and at the Byre Theatre, St Andrews, for the WYSIWYG International Children's Theatre Festival.

In 2010, Mark was awarded a distinction for his MLitt in Creative Writing at the University of Glasgow. The same year, he and poet Vicki Husband co-founded (and continue to co-host) the Glasgow Poetry Book Group. He is a member of the Glasgow-based poetry collective St Mungo's Mirrorball, and benefitted from their mentorship scheme in 2012-13 under the late, great Alexander Hutchison. Mark won the 2020 Magma Poetry Judge's Prize, and his poems have appeared in many magazines, including Shearsman, Stand, Tears in the Fence, The Manchester Review, The Rialto, Blackbox Manifold, and Poetry Wales.